Sales Leadership Journal

Sales Leadership Journal

ISBN: 9780981912639

Journal layout and design by Andrew Stebbins.

CODY ROCK PRESS   PHILADELPHIA

Introduction to this Journal

The single greatest factor determining your sales team's performance is not your CRM or other technology. It's certainly not the quality and depth of your marketing materials. It's not even you and your sales management prowess.

It is how they see and think about *what* and *why* they do what they do.

In other words, your sales team is primarily driven to perform by its mindsets — what they do — and how they think about what they do — with or without supervision. Since they're in the field most of the time (you hope), it's impossible for you to keep watch of their every move. After all, they are mature professionals. Sure, you can assign them specific tasks, but what really determines whether or not they succeed?

The short answer: It's all in their approach, and their approach starts in that space between their ears.

In everything they do, your team should consider these questions:

- How should I approach new opportunities?
- How well do I understand my marketplace?
- Do I realize how fluid it is? Am I staying in touch?
- What's changing my buyers' behavior?
- How should I approach discussions about price?

How they answer these and other key questions provides great insight on whether your team is predisposed to "doing the right things right." For example, a team that approaches negotiations with the correct mindset always seeks to proactively create value for prospects and customers in ways that go *beyond* price.

While you can train people to be more aware and intentional with these concepts, what you really want to know is whether they naturally think this way.

In other words, it's all about mindset — sales mindsets. These point to the approach sales professionals take in pursuing their day-to-day tasks, the on-the-ground work that builds relationships and closes meaningful deals. There are seven of them: marketplace awareness, negotiating, prospecting, product knowledge, sales acumen, account management, and business acumen. Top-performing sales teams manifest these mindsets in everything they do.

For example, think about the prospecting mindset. Does your team naturally look for the best new best opportunities, or do they wait for your lead-generation engine to point them in the right direction? Can they tell you what the ideal sales path looks like? Sales teams with a prospecting mindset always align their inner game with their actual game in day-to-day selling.

As you come to understand your team's mindsets, you'll begin to understand what comes naturally to them, and what needs work.

Of course, you might wonder whether you can develop something that doesn't come naturally in the first place. Our sense and experience is that a person's mindset is informed by their skill set. For example, a basketball player may be lousy at passing because they don't know how to handle the ball, or know how to anticipate where their teammates will be down the court. A good coach however, can help that player improve by building on their desire to help the team win.

When performance isn't optimal, the first question leaders face is whether the problem lies with skill or will. Many times, the answer is interrelated — a lack of skill leads to a lack of **will** or vice versa.

Once that's been determined, addressing the challenge requires a combination of knowledge, skill development, practice and metrics. Especially metrics. Measuring your team's progress is critical to improving its performance.

The fact is, too often salespeople get into a rut thinking that their job is solely about "showing up and talking about their stuff." But that's wrong. As a buyer, I don't need to hear about your product's specs, because I can get that information from your website. To succeed, salespeople need to offer customers some unique value — aligning themselves and their products to what the customer really needs.

When companies throw skills training or new apps at their team, they often succeed only in overloading them. As a result, teams absorb and use little of the new tools in which their companies have spent so much money.

The seven sales mindsets are simple and "obvious" — but require the effective help of sales managers to improve a team's performance. This Leadership Journal details these mindsets and offers helpful hints and idea-starters throughout. We've also given you plenty of space to make notes, brainstorm your best ideas and otherwise plan your greatest success yet.

With our best wishes,

Jose Palomino
CEO, Value Prop Interactive

Quick Journal Index

2

4

22

Mindset 1: Prospecting

A Commitment to Relentlessly Pursue New Opportunities

You already know how difficult it is to consistently meet — let alone, exceed — your goals if your sales team struggles to identify and win new business. Sure, you can sometimes make your numbers by relying primarily on your largest accounts, but that's not a strategy for long-term growth and success.

To improve outcomes, you simply must cultivate the prospecting mindset of your sales team. While this can be challenging, you can achieve this once you understand exactly what this mindset is — and whether your sales team has one.

Simply put, the prospecting mindset is an attitude that leads sales professionals to *always* look for their next opportunity. You might expect them to do this naturally— after all, prospecting is a basic component of the sales process. But in reality, few salespeople really prospect in a way that builds a continuously healthy sales pipeline.

One reason is that salespeople, like other professionals, can get comfortable. They may form habits of calling the same list of prospects and visiting the same group of customers. Following these paths, they pick up incremental revenue and may even hit their numbers. But at the end of the day, they're coasting to a degree, and that won't drive meaningful growth for your company.

This is why top sales teams are set apart by their commitment to prospecting. They have a passion for seeking fresh opportunities, and not only by being constantly on the lookout for new prospects. Those who stay closely attuned to their current customers' needs and interests — for example, recognizing when clients face a new problem that your products can solve — are using their prospecting mindset to maintain a *situational awareness* that makes them more effective at identifying and targeting opportunities.

While traditional benchmarks — the percentage of new opportunities compared to existing ones, for instance — measure prospecting success, they don't identify the presence of the prospecting mindset.

To do that, you have to ask these questions about each member of your team:

- Do they **intuitively ask** for referrals?
- Are they **actively and strategically hunting** for next-level sales opportunities? For example, do they identify new markets by region, industry or type of business?
- Do they attend conferences with the idea of **intentionally meeting** new people?
- Do they **take initiative** and look for opportunities on their own, or do they rely on your company's lead generation?
- Are they **aware of other buying centers** within their customer accounts? Maybe they've got Operations locked up. So, what about Logistics? Or HR? Or Finance?

If you answer "no" to any of these questions, it's likely that your team lacks a prospecting mindset — it's up to you to change that.

Of course, that's easier said than done. Anyone experienced in sales management knows that incentives impact sales culture. However, changing your compensation plan to better reward new opportunities is a long-term proposition. In the short term, though, offering some immediate rewards (money, iPads, vacations) for key *net-new* wins would send a strong signal that such opportunities are a priority.

By calling attention to and rewarding behaviors that reflect the prospecting mindset, you'll develop a culture that's better aligned to consistently meet — and exceed — your group's sales goals.

Mindset 2: Negotiation

A Commitment to Always Trade for Value

Since every negotiation is a give-and-take situation, it's never really a surprise when a sales professional quotes their best price and the client replies by asking for an even better one. That's why top-performing sales teams have a knack for uncovering and framing trade-offs based on true value to the customer rather than price alone.

These sales teams have a "**negotiating mindset.**" They understand the basic principles involved to avoid too quickly conceding on price or extraordinary requests that would be costly to deliver - and may not even be the root cause of a buyer's hesitancy.

When they have a negotiating mindset, sales professionals are able to shape deals without depending on unreasonable concessions on price or other matters. Even before they begin formal negotiations, they've thought about what they might offer — and what they might request — to shape a win-win agreement.

Sales professionals with this mindset understand that their discussions have to be framed at the beginning of the relationship, and not at the "closing table." Almost always, they propose options that are of lower cost to their company but of higher value to the customer. For example, they might offer to help develop their customer's go-to-market strategy, or give the customer regional exclusivity for a limited time. Neither impacts their product's price, but each certainly increases its value to the client.

Some say that sales negotiation is a form of game playing. The truth is that there is game theory at play. But the goal in B2B (long term relationships) selling should always be to create value for both your company and your customer, not employing "Jedi mind tricks" to win a round. That's just a shortcut to avoid thinking of solutions that can add to your true value to your customer.

This means *really* listening to all of your customer's needs from the first meeting until the contract is signed. For example, a customer's team may think your new product will be a headache to install. By offering real installation training, the salesperson assertively addresses a need that's not about pricing, but makes working with their company much more attractive… and profitable for all.

Assessing Your Team's Negotiating Mindset

As a sales manager, how can you tell if your team has a negotiating mindset? Start by looking at how many of your team's requests focus on price concessions. If it's a significant number, you've got work to do. But that's just the first step. Also ask yourself these questions:

- Does my sales team **align customer interests** with our products and services?
- Do they create **win-win solutions** with trade-offs that don't involve price?
- Can they **identify client motivations** and limitations?
- Are they able to **articulate our company's value** to overcome client objections?
- Can they **recognize the client's main ROI** considerations?

If the answer to any of these questions is "no," you need to strengthen your team's negotiating skills. Among the most effective ways to do this is to question every salesperson who argues that a major price break is needed to close a deal. Ask:

- "What **else** can we do for this customer?"
- "What are the customer's **three biggest challenges**?" The answer may offer hints of needs the sales person hasn't identified.
- "If instead of a price concession you had to inform the customer of a price increase, how would you **defend** it?"

When your team knows they'll be challenged on every price concession with questions like these, you'll influence the sales culture to think more proactively about creating value beyond price. Sales leaders should shape deals to increase revenue and margin … and value to the customer. By taking action to ingrain the negotiating mindset, you'll have more opportunities to raise profit margins and actually develop happier customers.

52

70

72

Mindset 3: Product Knowledge

A Commitment to KNOWING My Products

How well does your sales team know your products and services? Let's consider Ed, a hypothetical sales representative for a manufacturing firm. Word for word, he can recite his company's product brochure, right down to the specs for that axial-flow pump buried on the back page.

Despite his knowledge of the product, the deals Ed closes aren't anything special. Time and time again, he sells the same products to the same mid-level managers. As a sales manager, you have to wonder why. Simply put, Ed has an admirable grasp of product details, but not a **product knowledge mindset**.

His view is limited to what the brochure says about the products and how they work. With a real product knowledge mindset, Ed would understand his company's products and services so well that whatever problem a client faced, he could envision how his products would be the solution.

A product knowledge mindset is a broad understanding of how a product actually *solves problems* and *creates value*. It's not simply a memorization of a brochure or technical specifications. With it, salespeople bring in deals that are more creative, more complex and more valuable both to the company and the customer.

To determine if your sales teams has a product knowledge mindset, ask yourself these questions:

- Does your sales team present deals with **creative applications** of your products — ones that aren't obvious from the sales sheet?
- Does it actively engage with your technology resources to **create new ways** to solve a customer's problem?
- Do you see sales that offer a **combination of your products** as a way to address customer pain points?
- Does your team find **follow-on business** after the sale?

If you conclude that your team needs help developing this mindset, try these approaches:

- Publicly praise examples of product knowledge in action. For example, use weekly sales meetings to call out the people who put together creative, complex, larger deals.
- Check product knowledge, especially among new hires, by asking the team to answer 10 true or false questions about your products.
- Get the team together for an in-person discussion examining non traditional uses for your products.

Once you have your sales team putting real product knowledge to use, you will experience several desirable outcomes:

- Your customers will have greater respect for your salespeople. They won't mind educating your team about their business, because they know your company is focused on finding a way to solve their problems.
- When you launch new products, you can be confident that your team will absorb their potential and leverage them quickly.
- Most importantly, your sales team will have more confidence that they can make more money — always a powerful motivator.

Salespeople with a product knowledge mindset exhibit a hunger to understand how else their products can be used. For example, they pay close attention to case studies in order to glean new ideas. They question colleagues to learn from their experiences. Over time, they're able to quickly make connections between their products and a customer's pain points.

Mindset 4: Sales Acumen

A Commitment to the Craft

Since every deal follows a (often poorly) defined process, the sales team that knows how to move them forward closes more agreements and brings in more revenue. Seasoned sales managers recognize this, so when hiring they look for salespeople who understand basic blocking and tackling. Put another way, they hire people with a **sales acumen mindset**.

Sales acumen shouldn't be confused with "people skills." Gregariousness and charisma are positive qualities in a sales professional, but they aren't necessarily qualities the *entire* team or every professional can acquire.

Instead, sales acumen is a mindset that forms the basic underpinnings of sales success. Salespeople with this kind of insight can be counted on to not only understand the steps in the sales process, but to recognize how to advance through each one to closure.

As a sales manager, you're probably familiar with the marks of sales acumen. A sales professional with this mindset:

- Understands the **principles of lead generation** and how to ferret out new sales opportunities.
- Exhibits good **discovery** skills.
- Asks **smart** questions.
- Is savvy enough to **probe** without breaking rapport.
- Can **read an organization** and differentiate between low-level functionaries, high-level decision makers, and all the variants in between.
- Breaks down a sales opportunity into **stages**.
- Understands **where they are** in the process and what needs to happen next.
- Creates **urgency**.
- **Negotiates** effectively.
- Creates **win-win** situations.
- **Closes** business.

In essence, sales acumen is the understanding of time, people and value and how they fit into the sales process. So, when they have this mindset, sales teams are ultimately process-oriented. They're able to quickly size up an opportunity, recognize the players and understand how to create value. Perhaps even more critically, they have a firm grasp of everyone's timeline — both their own organization's and the prospect's — and they know how to knock down obstacles on both sides.

It's easy to recognize whether your team members need help developing their sales acumen. If any of the following concepts ring a bell, you're faced with knowledge gaps and need to take action.

- You're always addressing steps in the sales process at a remedial level. Teams with sales acumen don't require constant education on how to conduct sales activities.
- You routinely help your salespeople with tasks such as breaking down who's who in the prospect's organization or determining the stages of an opportunity.
- **Opportunities frequently get stuck**. Too many prospects "stuck" for too long is a sure sign that your team has challenges with deal advancement.
- Your team regularly asks for price concessions.
- Your team consistently fails to knock down obstacles, either internally or with the customer.

How do you address these issues? One way is to establish a baseline for skills and expectations in these areas, then hire for those qualities.

You can also help your team develop their mindset by taking advantage of a number of sales-training methods. Firms like Value Prop, Miller Heiman, Holden, SPIN and Sandler can develop your team's sales acumen in ways that show consistent results.

One last thought: The more structured and mature your sales operation is — you use a CRM, conduct weekly pipeline meetings and work within a formal negotiation framework, for example — the more your top performers will effortlessly map into these processes. As for those with knowledge gaps, these frameworks will help them mature and increase their level of success.

104

120

Mindset 5: Account Management

A Commitment to Fully Manage the Details

All sales managers know that current customers can be important sources of new revenue. But exactly how do sales professionals unlock fresh opportunities within existing accounts? The answer's really not surprising: They develop long-term relationships with key clients. Sales teams that excel at cultivating relationships are more likely to meet ongoing customer needs, uncover new opportunities with current clients, and increase the overall value for both parties over time.

The most successful salespeople understand this. They know that relationship building is about more than simply fulfilling requests for additional brochures or taking re-orders for established products.

Part of it is providing good customer service, of course. But the foundation lies within what we call the **account management** mindset.

Salespeople with account management mindsets are unique hybrids. They're both customer-centric — always looking to meet the needs of the customer — and sales-oriented — always looking for opportunities to grow new revenue from customers they already have.

As a sales manager, how do you evaluate your team's account management mindset? By recognizing its key indicators. High customer satisfaction, strong year-over-year account growth, and the absorption of new products by current accounts. These are all signs that your team understands the principles of account management and are applying them on a day-to-day basis.

If you don't see this happening, then look for these warning signs:

- Customers consistently say they **don't need to buy any more** of your company's products.
- You're rolling out new and interesting products or services, but **clients don't show interest** in trying them out. When this regularly occurs, your account manager may not be communicating closely enough with the customer.
- Rather than making the effort to care for existing customers, your sales team is overly **focused on new transactions**.
- Your team is afraid to push relationships, and is **frequently on the defensive** with clients.

If any of this sounds familiar, your team needs guidance and training.

You can help them develop an account management mindset by conducting these exercises:

- Ask each team member to create a snapshot of an account management plan. Along with the customer's current key stakeholder, be sure they name two or three additional stakeholders they're targeting within the organization.
- Have account managers name three challenges that have recently appeared on the radar of their top customers — even if they won't be solved by your products. This will tell you whether your team is truly paying attention to what's happening with their customers.
- Ask where they see a fit for all of your product lines within each account, regardless of whether they have the relationships in place to support those fits. This will illuminate the gaps between what your sales person has to offer and what the customer could be buying.

These exercises will help your team gain clarity about each of their accounts. With that insight, they can create more effective account management plans and develop more rewarding relationships with current customers.

136

142

Mindset 6: Business Acumen

A Commitment to Being a Business Peer

Two of the most effective ways to achieve sales growth are to sell more of your solutions to larger firms, or work with higher-level people at smaller organizations. Thus, to meet or exceed revenue targets, sales managers and their teams must continually navigate corporate hierarchies on the path toward growing their accounts.

That means your sales team must become experts at creating the kind of leverage that allows them to sell to higher and higher levels of management.

In short, they need to arrive at the client's office prepared to act as *business professionals* ready to provide consultative services, not simply as *salespeople* carrying slick brochures.

The difference between the two is as stark as night and day, and it matters. How your sales team presents itself determines how much time the prospect will spend with them and how much detail they will share about their business challenges.

When salespeople can leverage their business acumen, they talk with clients as peers. By being smart about business issues and sensitive to customer challenges, they'll develop the credibility needed to gain access to high-level decision-makers at their target companies. Without access to the C-suite, the deals they'll close are likely to be much smaller, making it more difficult for them to grow the account.

When you see more opportunities being driven to higher executive levels, you know your team has business acumen. For example, if your team once closed deals with the heads of plant operations, but now talk frequently with vice presidents of operations, they're moving upward through the hierarchy.

By contrast, salespeople who are continually pushed down to subordinates probably aren't being perceived as serious business professionals.

Business acumen is something you can help your team develop, though the process is sometimes like nailing Jello to a tree. Usually acquired through formal education and experience, business acumen isn't easy to teach. That said, consider these practical methods sales managers can use:

- Hold monthly "lunch and learn" sessions. Give your team a homework assignment, such as reading an article or watching a TED Talk on a topic that's important to your industry or the broader business world. Don't focus on your own products. Use the time over sandwiches to discuss the subject in detail.

- Ask the sales team to research their top prospects and describe what the companies do. Then, have them articulate the top three business challenges each prospect faces. These activities will both build your team's knowledge of business issues and teach them how to connect to the prospect's key obstacles.

- To embed this kind of behavior in day-to-day client interaction, regularly reinforce expectations that your team must understand each customer and its business environment. Set the bar high by insisting that all team members research the companies they call on. They should be familiar with all available public information and news coverage, and particularly anything that's appeared in major business publications like The Wall Street Journal.

These tactics will help your team approach more client meetings as business experts. When they do, they'll contribute greater value and gain deeper trust among both prospects and customers. By using their business acumen, they'll no longer come to the table as simple information providers, but as partners with valuable insights worth sharing.

156

Mindset 7: Marketplace Awareness

A Commitment to KNOWING My Marketplace

Most sales teams have a reasonably good grasp of their competition. They're able to rattle off the key differences between solutions and explain why their product is the best. But top-performing sales teams take their knowledge further: They understand their industry's ecosystem and recognize how outside forces can impact both their products and their customers.

Current trends play an essential role in shaping how consumers view products, and often dictate whether tomorrow's customers will buy more or less of what your company has to offer. Thus, a keen sense of the marketplace gives your sales team a powerful advantage.

Marketplace awareness is especially important because macro trends are often effective predictors of long-term demand. For example, think about Kodak in the late 1990s. Its leadership was so focused on their main competitor, Fuji, they missed the rapid changes in technology that made digital cameras possible. As a result, the one-time giant was largely unprepared when its film business began to slide. While sales cannot compensate for poor executive vision, it must nonetheless see "down the road" and adapt.

You can evaluate your team's understanding of macro trends and their impact simply by asking a few questions and listening carefully to the answers. To facilitate the conversation, try these ideas:

- Hold a postmortem to discuss recent sales losses and listen to the way your team describes each situation. If your salespeople can talk about the reasons for a loss in **precise terms**, they probably have good marketplace awareness.
- Similarly, a sales professional who understands that a loss resulted from either a competitor's actions or a change in the customer's situation is **paying attention** to events in the market.
- Look for signs that the team is **closely following industry events** and global trends. Have they taken the time to prepare strategies for dealing with your competition in light of them?
- Try asking these pointed questions: **Can you name each of our competitors**? How well can you articulate our company's strengths and weaknesses versus each competing firm? Can you describe the market's historical biases toward our products?

If your team fails to demonstrate marketplace awareness, there are several ways to help them develop it.

- Routinely challenge your team to be sure they have a holistic view of both competitors and trends.
- Make sure your people are asking customers meaningful questions. For example, which competitors are your customers considering, and why?
- Help develop sharp answers to competitive threats. While sales teams at larger corporations often get reports from their marketing teams, those at smaller organizations will need to conduct their own competitive research.

Pursuing market and competitive research is something all salespeople should be able to do. To keep themselves informed, have your team:

- Take advantage of information available on competitors' websites.
- Explain to customers and prospects that they'd like to better understand their organization and the marketplace. Have them probe to learn more about your competitors' strengths and weaknesses.
- Create a Google news alert for each of your competitors, prospects and customers, as well as for the top keywords about your industry. This is an easy, low-cost way to keep up with marketplace developments.
- Look for market research on your industry. Analysts such as Gartner and Forrester examine new products and technologies before they enter the marketplace, and can provide intelligence about what's coming down the pipeline.
- Regularly read both the general business and trade media.

Simply put, it's not enough to know who your direct competitors are. Sales professionals can only effectively position your products and services if they constantly monitor the marketplace for changes, disruptions and competitive moves.

Why Mindsets? Why Visual Thinking Tools?

While a wide scope of sales skills have been well documented, that very wealth of information makes it all the more difficult for sales leaders and professionals to absorb. Sales managers need to determine how to address their team's challenges with a smaller, more focused set of metrics and tools. They need to keep it simple. Otherwise, they risk overwhelming their team and themselves.

That's what our **Visual Thinking Tools** are all about.

Everything we do to accelerate sales is right-sized, so it's easily absorbed. We accomplish this by being visual. Everything the sales professional does day-to-day — managing time, for instance, or prioritizing accounts, or planning out their territory — is translated into **memorable and easy-to-use diagrams** that they can easily digest and put to use. In short, we offer sales training that's tailored to the way salespeople work and think.

Our approach was designed by salespeople, *for salespeople*. With it, your sales team will quickly learn to break down their skill sets in a way that allows them to prospect, negotiate and build relationships more intelligently and effectively. The results will be more deals closed, throughout more departments and at higher levels of customer organizations.

You won't just be managing a team of salespeople. Instead you'll lead a group of business professionals who discover and build relationships that customers trust and rely on, so your company develops greater loyalty — and sells more of your products to more customers.

www.VisualSellingTools.com

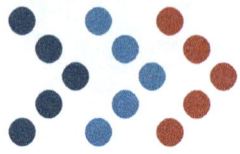

ValueProp | *Better Messaging.*
Better Sales.

www.ingramcontent.com/pod-product-compliance
Lightning Source LLC
Chambersburg PA
CBHW081341190326
41458CB00018B/6065

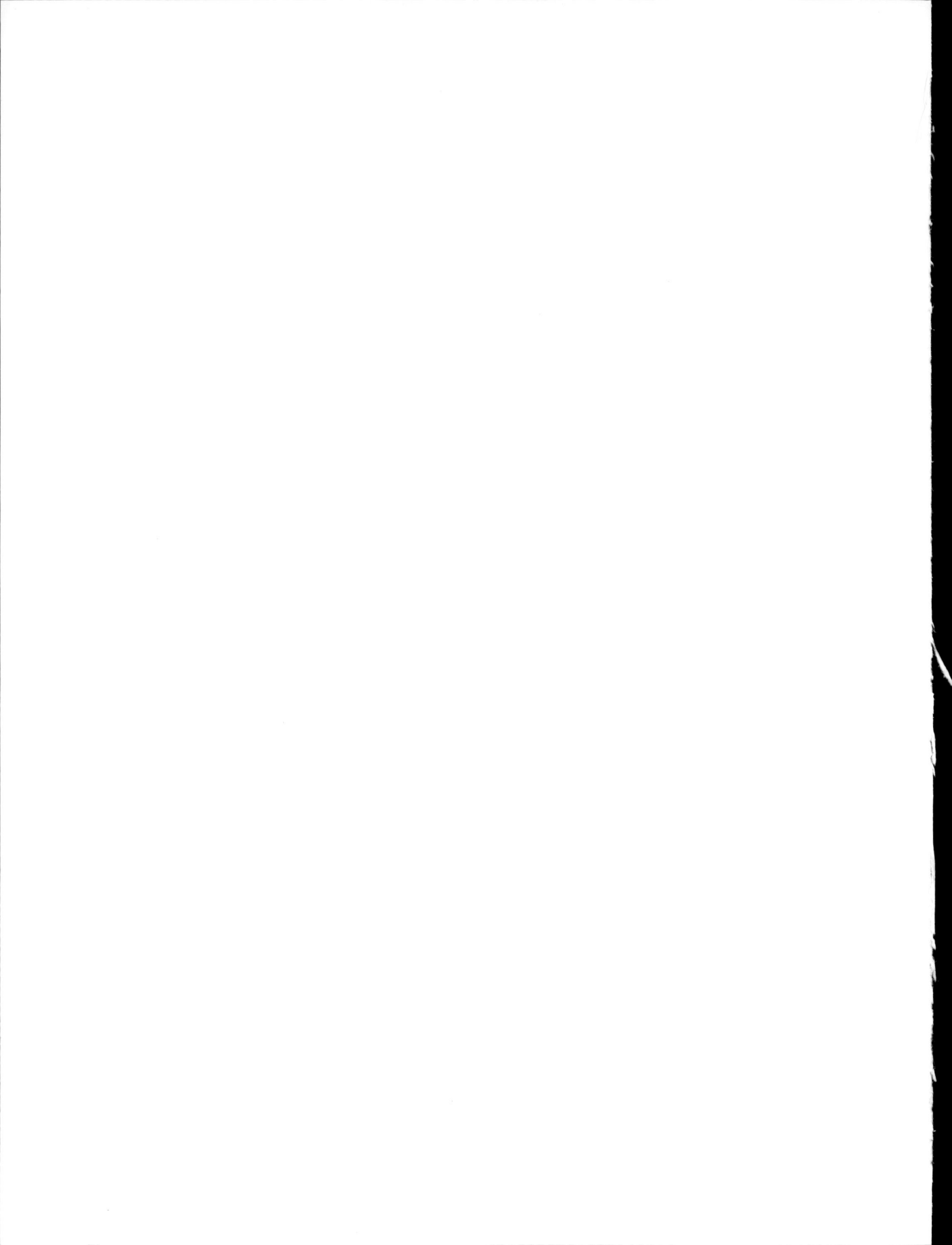